Musical Theory, Reading, Writing, Science, Health, Research, Drama, Singing, and Art

Music with Feelings

Mary K. Payne
B.S., M.S., SP Ed.

Music Lesson Plans for Teachers With or Without Musical Experience

All Rights Reserved. No part of this book may be used or reproduced by any means, graphic, electronic, or mechanical, including photocopying, recording, taping, or by any information storage retrieval system without the written permission of the author except in the case of brief quotations embodied in critical articles or reviews. For more information contact the author kathpayne@gmail.com.

Originally published by:
Kalliope Rising Press
P.O. Box 23
Burnet, Texas 78611

Copyright © 2018 by Mary K. Payne
Cover & Interior Design by Marcha Fox
Stock Photo Credit www.123rf.com/profile_yuyuyi'>yuyuyi
First Printing 2018

ISBN-13: 978-0-9980789-8-4

Publisher's Cataloging-In-Publication Data
(Prepared by The Donohue Group, Inc.)

Names: Payne, Mary K.
Title: Music with feelings : music lesson plans for teachers with or without musical experience / Mary K. Payne, B.S., M.S., SP Ed.
Description: Burnet, Texas : Kalliope Rising Press, [2018] | For instructors of elementary school age children. | "Musical Theory, Reading, Writing, Science, Health, Health Research, Drama, Singing, and Art."
Identifiers: ISBN 9780998078984 | ISBN 9780998078991 (ebook)
Subjects: LCSH: Music--Instruction and study--Outlines, syllabi, etc. | Elementary school teaching.
Classification: LCC MT10 .P39 2018 (print) | LCC MT10 (ebook) | DDC 372.87/044--dc23

Table of Contents

Introduction 1
Lesson 1: What is Music? 2
    ACTIVITY ONE: Learning Notes 4
    ACTIVITY TWO: Senses - Mixed 5
    ACTIVITY THREE: Acting and Singing 6
    ACTIVITY FOUR: Library Research 6
    ACTIVITY FIVE: Creative Writing 7
    ACTIVITY SIX: Making a Scrapbook 7
Lesson 2: Making Your Instruments Talk to You 9
    ACTIVITY ONE: What Am I? 13
    ACTIVITY TWO: Making Toy Instruments 14
    ACTIVITY THREE: Symphony Orchestra 15
    ACTIVITY FOUR: Playing the Toy Instruments 16
    ACTIVITY FIVE: Imitative Movements 18
    ACTIVITY SIX: Playing the Instruments 19
    ACTIVITY SEVEN: For Any Instrument 20
    ACTIVITY EIGHT: Go to Your Library 22
Lesson Three: Art With Music 24
    ACTIVITY ONE: Crayon Drawings 27
    ACTIVITY TWO: Singing the Boatman's Song 28
    ACTIVITY THREE: Row, Row, Row Your Boat 29
    ACTIVITY FOUR: Creative Writing 29
    ACTIVITY FIVE: Making Mobiles 29

ACTIVITY SIX: Painting to Music 30
ACTIVITY SEVEN: Instrument Soap Carving 31
Lesson Four: Songs For All Occasions 33
ACTIVITY ONE: Magic Song 35
ACTIVITY TWO: The Do Along Song 35
ACTIVITY THREE: For Spanish speakers 36
ACTIVITY FOUR: Halloween Songs 36
ACTIVITY FIVE: Thanksgiving Song 39
ACTIVITY SIX: Christmas Song 40
ACTIVITY SEVEN: Health Song 40
Lesson Five: Music Loves Energy 42
ACTIVITY ONE: Scrapbooks 45
ACTIVITY TWO: Listening Exercise 45
ACTIVITY THREE: Rain, a Natural Resource 46
ACTIVITY FOUR - Energy Poems 49
Resources to Help with Lessons 51
Miscellaneous Ideas 51
Warm-ups 52
Rhythm Band Instruments 52
About the Author 54

Introduction

The purpose of this music manual is to assist substitute teachers in their endeavor to teach music classes. Sometimes when music teachers are absent, the music classes are cancelled. To help eliminate this problem, this manual is geared towards the teachers who have limited music backgrounds. This manual has been written in the form of lesson plans, in order to make it easier for the teachers to read.

Music with Feeling deals with confluent education. This involves knowledge, affective, and skill objectives. *Knowledge* objectives usually deal with recalling facts. *Affective* objectives are meant to help the child who does poorly in the knowledge domain. Affective deals with empathizing, social participation, and value clarification. *Empathizing* deals with trying to get children to identify themselves with other people and objects. With activities involving empathizing, we try to rid children of their prejudices. *Social participation* is having the students become more involved with each other by working in teams or small groups. It also teaches them responsibility by having them choose roles within their groups. *Value clarification* involves discovering and clarifying a person's values. This manual was written in order to help children learn to appreciate music, and to see how music affects their lives.

Lesson 1: What is Music?

Intended Student Audience	3rd to 6th Grade
Suggested Time for Classroom Use of Material	4 Class Periods (120 minutes)
Materials for Classroom Use	Notebook

Objectives within the Cognitive Domain

Upon completion of this lesson the student will:

Knowledge

    a. Write the definition of music.
    b. Know the background and history of five composers.
    c. Write the lines and spaces of the Treble clef.
    d. Know the words and melody of a song.

Skill Development

    a. Explain the benefit of having music in our society.
    b. Take notes in class and put them in a music appreciation notebook.
    c. Collect data on music found in magazines, newspapers, etc., and put in a notebook.
    d. Sing or act out a song of their choice.
    e. Explain what they like or dislike about music.
    f. Collect data on composers.

Objectives within the Affective Domain

Upon completion of this lesson the student will:

Social Participation

    Be willing to work in small groups.

Empathizing

    Empathize with inanimate objects.

Teaching Suggestions/Lessons Overview

The purpose of this lesson is to get the children to have a better understanding of what music is all about. People usually do not like things that they are not familiar with. Children are the same way. The trick is to get them motivated.

There are a number of activities to choose from. Choose one that fits the personality of your class. Some children need activities that keep them active. Others enjoy quiet lecture-type discussions.

Mary K. Payne

Introducing the Lesson

The lesson should start by having everyone sing a song they all know. Encourage everyone to sing. Then ask the class, how do you suppose this song lasted for so many years? That is correct. Through the music that composers have written down through the years. The following points should be discussed:

1. Music is organized sound and movement. It is written and played according to rules.

2. Melody, rhythm, harmony, and form are the general names for these rules.

3. Music is sound that is pleasant to one's ears.

Implementing the Lesson

After discussing the fundamentals of music, play about four records that have different rhythms. Play a classical, hard rock, march, and folk song. The idea is to get the children interested.

Put the students in groups of five each. Then assign each group one of the following activities.

ACTIVITY ONE: Learning Notes

1. Write these mystery words on the board.

2. Now clap the rhythm.

Music with Feelings

ACTIVITY TWO: Senses - Mixed

Write these questions on the board and have the groups discuss them.

1. How does a note smell?
2. How does a guitar taste?
3. What does melody taste like?
4. How does singing taste?

Now have the students make some up.

ACTIVITY THREE: Acting and Singing

Have half of the students sing this while the other half acts it out.

Irish Song--Tune: *For He's a Jolly Good Fellow*

>1. My mother and father are Irish. (3 times)
>And I am Irish, too.
>2. Bought a sack of potatoes. (3 times)
>And they were Irish, too.
>3. We peeled them, we diced them, and we boiled them. (3 times)
>4. Invited all of the neighbors. (3 times)
>To eat the Irish stew.

ACTIVITY FOUR: Library Research

This activity can be for homework or done during class. Have each group choose one composer to do research on. Have them decide among themselves which person will write the paper. Then three students will do the research and turn it into the person who is having to lookup words and write the paper. The writer makes all the grammatical corrections. The fifth person will draw a picture of their composer.

After each group gets their paper written, the group decides whom they want to present their composition. The people who drew the pictures will then display them somewhere in the room.

The teacher should end this activity by having the children discuss answers to these questions in their groups.

1. Would you like to be a composer?
2. How do you think it would feel to be a composer?
3. What do you like or dislike about music?
4. What has music contributed to our society?
5. Write in your own words what music is.

ACTIVITY FIVE: Creative Writing

Begin your activity with these titles on the board:

1. If I Were A Drum
2. Once I Was The Strings In A Piano
3. The Joys Of Being A Sound
4. If I Was Rhythm
5. The Day I Rode Inside a Guitar

ACTIVITY SIX: Making a Scrapbook

Use this scrapbook activity for a homework project. Have the children collect pictures of instruments, articles written on music, etc. Also, have the creative writing papers mounted in your scrapbook. Use a large spiral notebook or giant tablet.

Concluding the Lesson

Have the children read some of their compositions out loud to the class. Discuss them and compare notes with each other.

Predicted Outcome

The products indicate the application of the knowledge. The participation is observed throughout as being a key factor in the success of the lesson. Empathizing is expressed both orally and written.

Lesson 2: Making Your Instruments Talk to You

Intended Student Audience	Lower & Upper Elementary
Suggested Time for Classroom Use of Material	One or Two Activities per 30 minute class periods
Materials for Classroom Use	Oatmeal boxes, wood, nails, coke caps, orange juice cans, pencils, spools, jars, corn, plastic fruit, coffee can, oil can, rice, bells, sandpaper, pie pans, metal, sticks, hammer, bamboo, elastic and children's instruments.

Objectives Within the Cognitive Domain

Upon completion of this lesson the students will:

Knowledge

    a. Know the name of ten instruments.
    b. Know the definition of rhythm, melody, harmony, and form.
    c. Know how to make toy instruments.

d. Know the background and history of different instruments.
e. Know the meaning of time signature.
f. Know the definition of a musician.
g. Know note value.

Skill Development

a. Make toy instruments.
b. Collect data on the instruments.
c. Classifying instruments.
d. Explain the importance of having instruments.
e. Play the toy instruments.
f. Identify note values in nature.
g. Collect data on sounds in nature.

Objectives Within the Affective Domain

Upon completion of this lesson the student will:

Social Participation

Be willing to work as a member of a small group.

Empathizing

a. Empathize with musicians.
b. Empathize with inanimate objects.

Teaching Suggestions/ Lesson Overview

This lesson deals with students discovering the different types of instruments and how they sound.

Also, most children have the idea that playing an instrument other than the drums or guitar makes you a "sissy". It is my intention to help the students who believe this to become more aware of the different instruments and the musicians who play them. For this lesson, the teacher will have to inquire as to where the instruments are kept at the school.

Introducing the Lesson

The best way to introduce a lesson on instruments is to play some for the students. If the teacher can play the piano or autoharp, so much the better. For the teacher who does not play, the tambourine, maracas, bell, triangle, or wood blocks will do just as well. The children love any instrument, especially the ones they can play. After the teacher plays a few of the instruments, she should ask some of the following questions.

1. Has anyone in this class ever played one of these instruments?

ANSWER: Answers will vary.

2. Does anyone know the names of these instruments?

ANSWER: Tambourine, triangle, wood blocks, recorder, drum, or any other instrument you bring.

3. Has anyone ever thought about being a musician in a symphony orchestra?

Mary K. Payne

ANSWER: Answers will vary.

4. What is a musician?

ANSWER: One who plays a musical instrument, or sings. They also compose music.

5. Does everyone know what a symphony orchestra is?

ANSWER: A symphony orchestra is a large group of musicians with a variety of instruments who play long pieces of music called symphonies.

6. What is rhythm?

ANSWER: Rhythm is movement or flow in which the sounds follow a regular pattern with accents or beats coming at a certain fixed time. Rhythm makes music move.

7. What is melody?

ANSWER: An arrangement of musical tones in a series so as to form a tune.

8. What is form?

ANSWER: Form is how a piece of music is put together.

9. What is harmony?

ANSWER: The sound of tones put together in such a way that is pleasing to hear.

Implementing the Lesson

Have someone who plays in the symphony come and speak to the class. Next, take the class on a field trip to see and hear a symphony.

Ask the students if anyone in their family plays an instrument. Suggest that they get their relatives to come and play for them.

Tell the students to bring all the materials to class to make the instruments.

Assign the students to work in one of five groups with an even number of students in each group. This type of interaction helps children learn to get along with each other.

Some of the activities are meant for fifth and sixth only. You should decide which ones to use with your children.

ACTIVITY ONE: What Am I?

Give each group a piece of paper with these riddles written on them.

1. I'm long and black and not very thick. And some children call me a licorice stick.

ANSWER: Clarinet

2. I'm round and fat and I go boom! I march in parades, so give me room.

ANSWER: Drum

3. You'll find me where the angels dwell; I'm made of shining gold. I can make a heavenly sound; but I'm very large to hold.

ANSWER: Harp

4. I have a bridge, but not over water, and a neck but not a head. If you don't want to practice three hours a day, you'd better play games instead.

ANSWER: Can be violin, viola, cello, or bass violin.

5. I'm made of wood and have four strings. It takes a bow to make me sing.

ANSWER: Can be violin, viola, cello, or bass violin.

Have the children answer the riddle and then role-play their instrument. Have the class try to guess what they are. Have one child be the instrument and the other child is the musician playing the instrument.

ACTIVITY TWO: *Making Toy Instruments*

The teacher will have to bring materials with her or ask them to bring the materials with them for the next class time. Divide the group up according to how many working areas you have available.

1. Make drums out of oatmeal boxes. Use a spool on a pencil for a mallet. Or use a coffee can with lid, covered with construction paper.

2. Make jiggle clog out of a piece of wood with coke caps nailed on it.

3. Shakers can be made from any of the following:

>a. Can with beans in it and a spool to close the hole.
>b. Jars covered with contact paper and corn inside.

c. Orange juice cans covered with tape and colored paper, with corn inside.
d. Plastic fruit with rice inside with a pencil stuck in the hole.
e. Oil can with rice or corn inside.
f. Pie pans stuck together with staples and corn inside.

4. Make sand blocks out of two pieces of wood with one side covered with sandpaper.

5. Make a triangle using metal with nails.

6. Make a bracelet out of elastic and sew bells onto it. Put bells on the end of a stick.

7. Use bamboo for sticks.

NOTE: Making instruments is not the musical experience, using them is.

ACTIVITY THREE: Symphony Orchestra

The teacher should begin by explaining the following, using pictures.

There are four sections in the symphony orchestra. They are as follows:

1. Strings - violin, viola, cello, double bass, and harp.

2. Woodwinds - piccolo, flute, oboe, clarinet, English horn, and bassoon.

3. Brass - cornet, trumpet, French horn, trombone, and tuba.

4. Percussion - celesta, bells, chimes, xylophone, timpani, snare drum, bass drum, castanets, cymbals, triangles, and gongs.

5. Other instruments are sometimes called in for modern compositions, such as the saxophone.

The strings, brass, and woodwind choirs play the melody, and the percussion section plays rhythmic effects. You can play melodies with the xylophone, chimes, and celesta, but they are seldom used for such purposes.

Now the teacher should divide the children up into four groups. Give each group one of the sections of the orchestra. Have them decide which instrument they want to research. They can do one of the following:

a. Write a report on their instrument.

b. Draw a picture of their instrument.

c. Make a toy or model to illustrate.

d. Write a creative writing paper with such titles as:

    1. The Day I Ate a Tuba
    2. How I Became a Bell
    3. I Wish I Were a (n) *"any instrument"*

e. Put on a play by having each person represent an instrument. Have the children write the play, or just use the percussion instruments as sound effects.

ACTIVITY FOUR: *Playing the Toy Instruments*

The teacher should pass out the toy instruments and then put the children in a certain seating arrangement. Before they play their instruments, there are a few activities that they should go through in order for them to be read to keep their beat in the toy orchestra.

Activity A: Note Value - Movement

1. The teacher should teach the value of the quarter note, half note, and whole note.

2. Then explain the time signature, which is going to be 4/4. Each eighth note gets one-half of a beat. Each quarter note gets on beat. Each half note gets two beats. Each whole note gets four beats. We start with quarter notes, because a child learns to walk to quarter notes, as it seems more natural.

3. Have the children walk around the room to quarter notes. Have them clap and count at the same time.

4. Have them do the same with half and then whole notes. Do the eighth note last.

5. Now parallel the notes with an animal, and act it out.

   a. eighth note - horse
   b. quarter note - rabbit
   c. half note - kangaroo
   d. whole note - elephant

Activity B: Class Discussion

Which note would you like to be and why?

Activity C: Nature Walk

1. Divide into groups.

2. Listen for sounds of machines, rain, wind blowing, children running, etc. Identify the beat.

3. See which group collects the most sounds.

Activity D: Rhythms in Nature

Discuss the rhythms in music as related to rhythm in nature. Examples: pulse of heart beat, the regularity of the years, hours, days, tide changes, seasons, and in poetry. Read two poems as examples.

Example 1

> Mary had a little lamb,
> A little veal, a steak
> An omelet, and some chocolate pie.
> She couldn't eat the cake.

Example 2

> Mary, Mary, quite contrary,
> You always disagree.
> If I say, "Two and Two is Four,"
> You're bound to say, "It's Three."

ACTIVITY FIVE: Imitative Movements

For Upper Grades

1. Think of all the machines in the world that have a steady rhythm to them. This includes hammers, wheels, pistons, and trains.

2. Now act it out.

Music with Feelings

For Lower Grades

1. Think of all the toys you can. For example: toy soldiers, dolls, and rocking horses. Now choose partners. One partner can be wind-up toy, and then they can change places.

2. Play follow the leader using the following movements: marching, walking, skipping, hopping, galloping, arm movement, head movement, leg movement all in equally rhythmic movements.

ACTIVITY SIX: *Playing the Instruments*

1. Have children pick the instruments they want to play.

2. Put the children in the proper places.

Instrument Seating Arrangement

			Drums	
		Finger Cymbals		
	Bells		Maracas	
Sticks	Castanets		Sand Blocks	
	Jingle Clogs			Gongs
Cymbals	Wood Blocks		Tambourines	

TEACHER

3. Use the song *Yankee Doodle*.

   Yan-keep Doo-dle went to town a rid-ing on a po-ny.
   He stuck a feath-er in his hat and called it mac-a-roni.

Mary K. Payne

Chorus:
Yan-kee Doo-dle keep it up, Yan-kee Doo-dle Dandy,
Mind the mu-sic and the step and let the girls be han-dy.

4. Have the children sing the song all together.

5. Have one-half the children sing the verse and the other half sing the chorus.

6. Have them walk and clap to the music.

7. Have them whistle the song.

8. Have whole class think first line and sing the last four words.

9. Now point to the instruments you want played on each beat.

10. Have the drums play once all the way through the song.

11. Have half of the class singing at all times. There will probably not be enough instruments for everyone, anyway.

ACTIVITY SEVEN: *For Any Instrument*

Sing and play sticks to the tune of "*When the Saints Go Marching In.*" Sticks can be changed to any instrument.

Oh, when we play (tap, tap)
Our rhythm sticks (tap, tap)
Oh, when we play our rhythm sticks.
Oh, don't you want to come and join us
When we play our rhythm sticks. (tap, tap)

Oh, when we play (tap, tap)
Our tambourines (tap, tap)
Oh, when we play our tambourines

Music with Feelings

Oh, don't you want to come and join us
When we play our tambourines.

Oh, when we play (tap, tap)
Our triangle (tap, tap)
Oh, when we play (boom, boom)
Our big bass drums (boom, boom) etc.

Concluding the Lesson

How would it feel to ride inside of your instrument all day long? Have them tell each other. Pick up all the instruments and have the children discuss how it felt to be part of an orchestra.

Predicted Outcome

Rhythm instruments help a child to learn the beat. One of the greatest contributions to the physical growth of children is the opportunity rhythms give for gaining muscular coordination and control. Children, who want to play their instrument, really try harder to make the movements necessary to play it correctly. This is why we walked and clapped first, in order to get them ready to play their instruments in rhythm.

ACTIVITY EIGHT: Go to Your Library

Check out slides on any of the following instruments. A Symphony Orchestra consists of four families:

1. Brass Section

    a. trumpet
    b. trombone
    c. French horn (rich mellow tone)
    d. tuba

2. Percussion Section

    a. celesta (organ-type piano)
    b. snare drum
    c. bass drum
    d. kettle drums (timpani) pedal is used to raise and lower the pitch
    e. cymbals
    f. gong (provides oriental or supernatural effect)
    g. wood block (tapping)
    h. castanets (Spanish music), tambourine
    i. maracas (Spanish or Latin effect)
    j. orchestra bells

3. String Section

    a. harp (47 strings, 6 1/2 octaves, 7 pedals)
    b. bass viola
    c. cello
    d. viola (2 inches longer and thicker than violin, 5 tones lower)
    e. violin

4. Woodwind Section

    a. piccolo (blow across opening)
    b. flute

c. bass clarinet
d. clarinet (singular reed)
e. saxophone
f. oboe
g. English horn (double reed)
h. bassoon (nasal tone)
i. contra bassoon

Lesson Three: Art With Music

Intended Student Audience	Lower Elementary
Suggested Time for Classroom Use of Material	Each activity takes 30 minutes
Materials for Classroom Use	Recorded music, pencil, tablet, crayons, Boatman's Song, art paper

Objectives Within the Cognitive Domain

Upon completion of this lesson the students will:

Knowledge

    Know the Boatman's Song.

Skill Development

    a. Draw a picture.
    b. Communicating how they feel in their artwork.
    c. Listening and interpreting skills.

Objectives Within the Affective Domain

Upon completion of this lesson the student will:

Social Participation

>Be willing to work as a member of a group.

Empathizing

>Empathize with people and inanimate objects.

Projection

>Project their personalities into their artwork.

Receiving

>Show a willingness to participate in the activities.

Responding

>a. Respond to the listening activities by listening to other recorded music and writing or drawing something reflecting the music.
>b. Develop their imagination.

Valuing

>a. Develop responsibility.
>b. Have more confidence.
>c. Develop trust.

Mary K. Payne

Teaching Suggestions/ Lessons Overview

This lesson will involve a study in a number of different subjects. The nature walk will involve an environmental study with music or sounds that nature makes.

This art lesson will be with crayons, because this age child does better with crayons. The children may repeat the same colors for the same objects. They really enjoy this freedom of expression.

This type of lesson reveals certain desires and conflicts a child may have. The child can express some of his major concerns. It also gives the child the opportunity to experience mastery and self-assurance, because in art there are no wrong answers. The child needs larger paper to give him more freedom to express himself.

The teacher must know how to sing or play in order to do activity one in its entirety. If they cannot sing or play, just have them do the art project using some of the motivation. Then do to activity three.

Introducing the Lesson

Start this lesson by playing or singing Boatman's Song. Sometimes it is better to announce the name of a song after you play it, because children listen more closely when they are trying to figure out what something is about.

ACTIVITY ONE: Crayon Drawings

Start the lesson by saying:

1. Listen to this song and try to figure out what it is all about.

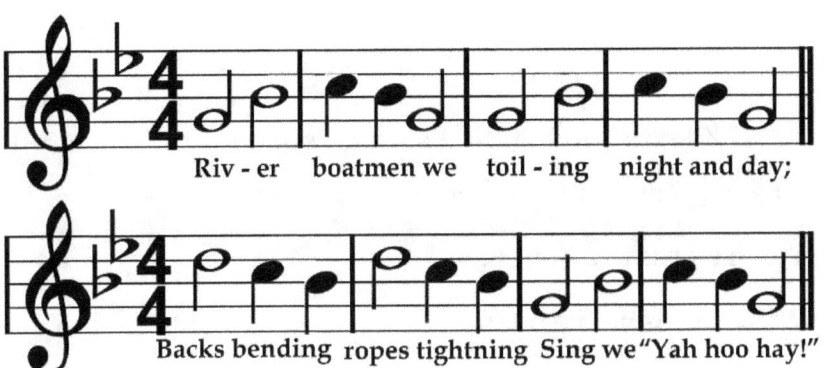

2. The name of that song is the *Boatman's Song*.

3. I want you to draw a picture using the title "If I Were A Boatman or Boatwoman."

4. How do you think it would feel to be a boatman?

5. Would you be big and strong or little and weak?

6. Would you be in a hurry?

7. Would you feel happy or sad?

8. Where are you? Are you in a boat, a store, or at home?

9. Can you hear anything outside or near you; like the ocean roaring, or the trees rustling in the breeze? How would it feel to be a tree?

10. Would you smell anything? Does the smell make you sick or is it sweet?

11. What kind of clothes would you wear? Would you wear a cowboy suit?

12. What color eyes and hair do you have?

ACTIVITY TWO: Singing the *Boatman's Song*

1. Sing the song to all the children.

2. Teach words to children.

3. Write words on the board.

4. Is the song fast or slow?

5. Have them tap the beat slowly.

6. Have them mouth the words silently.

7. Sing the melody while waving your hand to the beat of the music.

8. Place melody in air with hand. As the melody goes up, make the hand movement go up.

9. Listen and count the number of phrases in the song.

10. Let them try to sing it alone.

11. Sing it by groups.

12. Have them chant the words in rhythm.

13. Have one group dramatize the song, while the rest sing it.

Music with Feelings

ACTIVITY THREE: Row, Row, Row Your Boat

1. Sing to students.

2. Put words on the board.

3. Sing the song in rounds.

ACTIVITY FOUR: Creative Writing

1. Play the song while they write.

2. Place children into five groups.

3. Have the children decide who will be the secretary.

4. Have the children list ten things you have to have to be a boatman.

5. Have them write a short paragraph or story using their list.

ACTIVITY FIVE: Making Mobiles

1. Draw the instruments on poster board and cut them out.

2. Color both sides with markers.

3. Label the instruments.

4. Punch holes in top.

5. Cover clothes hangers with yarn.

6. Cross two clothes hangers and connect them with yarn.

7. Hang instruments with pipe cleaners made into circles or with yarn.

ACTIVITY SIX: Painting to Music

1. Play any music you want.

2. Ask the children how it makes them feel.

3. Tell them to close their eyes and listen to the music. Then ask them what do you see?

4. What colors does that remind you of?

5. Now, paint what you see or hear.

Concluding the Lesson

Activity six is a good concluding activity for this unit. It is important for the children to see the relationship music has with art.

Predicted Outcome

The students will relax and learn to enjoy music while they do something they already like to do. I have never seen a child who does not like to color or paint. The children will associate fun with music, and maybe they will start liking music more. Most of the younger children already like music classes, but the older children sometimes get bored. They feel ridiculous singing these songs that are in most of the music books. Until a music book is printed that is composed of modern songs, I intend to put activities in my manual that will appeal to all elementary children.

ACTIVITY SEVEN: Instrument Soap Carving

1. Use Ivory Soap for the carving.

2. Play music that has only instruments and no vocal part in it.

3. Tell them to pick which instrument they want to carve.

4. Show them some pictures of the instruments they choose.

5. Assign this as a home project, because we would not like the children to bring knives to school.

Mary K. Payne

Concluding the Lesson

Have the children display all their paintings on a bulletin board with the title "Art With Music" to surprise their teacher when she gets back from being absent.

Predicted Outcome

The children will have an art lesson and at the same time enjoy a music experience. It is very seldom a person can do both. One subject might inspire the other.

Lesson Four: Songs For All Occasions

Intended Student Audience	Lower & Upper Elementary
Suggested Time for Classroom Use of Material	Allow 30 minutes to teach one song
Materials for Classroom Use	Chalk and chalk board or song sheets

Objectives in the Cognitive Domain

Knowledge

    a. Know the tune of songs.
    b. Know how to read the words of songs.

Skill Development

    Dramatize some of the songs.

Mary K. Payne

Objectives Within the Affective Domain

Upon completion of this lesson the students will:

> a. Acquire a repertory of songs to be carried into their home and social life.
> b. Arrive at a conception of music as one of the beautiful and fun things of this life.
> c. Develop a love for music and acquire a taste for how to choose the music he listens to.

Teaching Suggestions/ Lesson Overview

The primary purpose of this lesson is for the students to get a chance to learn some songs with which they already are a little familiar.

Implementing the Lesson

Most of the songs in this unit are tunes most people know. The composers wrote words to go with tunes that people are familiar with. This way, the substitute will not be required to have the ability to read music.

The teacher will first sing the song to the children. Then put the words on the chalkboard or pass out some song sheets.

Music with Feelings

ACTIVITY ONE: Magic Song
Tune: Skip to My Lou

> Clap your hands and turn around.
> Clap your hands and bow to the ground.
> Touch your head and touch your chin
> Open the door and tip-toe in.

ACTIVITY TWO: The Do Along Song
Tune: Row, Row, Row Your Boat

(These are fun lyrics for Easter or Halloween, respectively.)

> Hop, hop, hop around
> Just like bunnies do
> Touch your toes
> Wiggle your nose
> You're a bunny, too!
>
> Skip, skip, skip around
> All around the room.
> Spread your arms and
> Fly back home
> Like witches on a broom.

ACTIVITY THREE: For Spanish speakers

The following song is for a teacher who can speak Spanish. It is a good way to teach a child to count to ten in Spanish.

>Uno, dos, tres gatitos
>Cuatro, cinco, seis gatitos
>Siete, ocho, neuve gatitos
>Diez gatitos son.
>
>Diez (10), nueve (9), ocho (8) gatitos
>Siete (7), cinco (5), seis (6) gatitos
>Cuatro (4), tres (3), dos (2) gatitos
>Uno (1) gatito es.

ACTIVITY FOUR: Halloween Songs

1. A Haunted House

Tune: Are You Sleeping?

>Tip-toe, tip-toe, tip-toe, tip-toe,
>Knock on the door, knock on the door
>Here comes Jack-O-Lantern
>Here comes Jack-O-Lantern
>Run, run, run;
>Run, run, run.

2. Jack O'Lantern

Tune: Are You Sleeping?

> Jack-O-Lantern, Jack-O-Lantern,
> Halloween, Halloween.
> See the witches flying
> Hear the winds sighing,
> Woo - oo - oo
> Woo - oo - oo!

3. Goblin in the Dark

Tune: Farmer in the Dell

> (1) The goblin in the dark,
> the goblin in the dark.
> Hi, Ho, On Halloween,
> The goblin in the dark.
>
> (2) The goblin calls a witch, etc.
> (3) The witch calls a bat, etc.
> (4) The bat calls a ghost, etc.
> (5) The ghost says, "Boo," etc.
> (6) They all scream and screech, etc.

4. Halloween's Coming

Tune: Are You Sleeping?

> Halloween's coming, Halloween's coming,
> What shall we do? What shall we do?
> We'll have a party, We'll have a party,
> That's what we'll do! That's what we'll do!

5. Halloween Time

Tune: Here We Go 'Round the Mulberry Bush

(1) I'm going to ride the witch's broom,
the witch's broom, the witch's broom.
I'm going to ride the witch's broom,
High up to the Moon.

(2) I'm going to be a big black cat,
a big black cat, a big black cat.
I'm going to be a big black cat,
hissing at everybody.

(3) I'm going to be a pumpkin round,
a pumpkin round, a pumpkin round.
I'm going to be a pumpkin round
rolling all over the town.

6. Boo!

Tune: Mary Had a Little Lamb

(1) We are pumpkins big and round,
Big and round, Big and round.
We are pumpkins big and round,
Sitting on the ground.

(2) See our great big shiny eyes,
Shiny eyes, Shiny eyes.
See our great big shiny eyes
Looking all around.

(3) See our great big laughing mouths,
Laughing mouths, laughing mouths.
See our great big laughing mouths,
Smiling right at you.

Music with Feelings

ACTIVITY FIVE: Thanksgiving Song

Tune: Here We Go 'Round the Mulberry Bush

Have the children act this out as they sing it.

(1) This is the way the Pilgrims walk,
the Pilgrims walk, the Pilgrims walk.
This is the way the Pilgrims walk
Thanksgiving Day in the morning.

(2) This is the way the Turkey struts,
the Turkey struts, the Turkey struts.
This is the way the Turkey struts
Thanksgiving Day in the morning.

(3) This is the way the Indians dance, etc.

(4) This is the way we all give Thanks, etc.
(slowly and sustained)

Refrain (after each verse)
Let us be glad and grateful today
Grateful today, grateful today.
Let us give thanks with joy today,
Thanksgiving Day in the morning.

Mary K. Payne

ACTIVITY SIX: Christmas Song
Tune: White Christmas

> I'm dreaming of a pink, purple,
> polka dotted Christmas
> Just like the ones I never had.
>
> Where the treetops break off,
> and children take off
> To hear car tires in the snow
> *(screeching sound here)*
>
> I'm dreaming of a pink, purple,
> polka-dotted Christmas
> With every Valentine I write.
>
> May your days be happy and new,
> And may all your Christmases
> be pin, purple, polka dotted, too.

ACTIVITY SEVEN: Health Song
Tune: Are You Sleeping?

> (1) Brush, brush, brush,
> Up, up, up.
> Lower teeth, lower teeth.
> Brush right after eating,
> That's the way to keep them
> Shining bright, healthy white.

(2) Brush, brush, brush,
Down, down, down,
Upper teeth, upper teeth.
Brush right after eating
That's the way to keep them,
Shining bright, healthy white.

(Repeat last line 3 times and hold)

Concluding the Lesson

Always end every class by singing a song.

Predicted Outcome

The children will have fun without having to put forth the effort to read the notes to music and to learn a new tune. They have a hard enough time reading the words much less having to learn a tune at the same time. So, try to pick a tune that almost everyone knows.

Lesson Five: Music Loves Energy

Intended Student Audience	5th Grade
Suggested Time for Classroom Use of Material	80 minutes
Materials for Classroom Use	Construction paper, rhythm band instruments, such as the cymbals, rhythm sticks, triangles, and sand blocks.

Objectives Within the Cognitive Domain

Upon completion of this lesson the students will:

Knowledge

    a. Illustrate a knowledge of how and why food chains are formed.
    b. Know the words and melody of a song.
    c. Know the names of the tunes.
    d. Write a poem using key energy words to go with a familiar tune.
    e. Know how rain provides energy.

Skill Development

    a. Explain the benefits of conserving energy.
    b. Collect pictures of things that use energy.
    c. Singing and acting skills.
    d. Compose a rain dance.
    e. Listen and identify different sounds that use energy.
    f. Memorization.
    g. Discriminated listening.
    h. Maintain rhythmic pattern.

Objectives Within the Affective Domain

Upon completion of this lesson the student will:

Social Participation

Be willing to work in small groups.

Empathizing

Empathize with inanimate objects.

Teaching Suggestions/ Lesson Overview

The purpose of this lesson is to get the children to have a better understanding of how important energy is to the people on this planet. This lesson can be taught in two 40 minute class sessions or broken up into four 20 minute lessons, depending on how musical the class is. It also depends on your children's reading level.

Introducing the Lesson

Begin the lesson by explaining how we need energy from the sun in order for all living things to exist on earth.

Implementing the Lesson

We will begin the learning activity by having a discussion on things that use energy, and where we get our sources of energy. When you get up in the morning, the radio alarm clock goes off, you turn on the lights, then you cook your breakfast, and then brush your teeth with a plastic toothbrush. Now what do these four things have to do with energy?

Music loves energy because it takes energy to make music. Whether it is from a radio, or the energy it takes to beat a drum, the sound or music it makes is energy.

Music with Feelings

Children remember ideas better when they are put to music. They love to chant little songs and it helps them remember the words.

ACTIVITY ONE: Scrapbooks

Collect pictures and articles pertaining to energy. Put some up on the bulletin board.

ACTIVITY TWO: Listening Exercise

Play a recording of sounds such as a train, automobile, motorcycle, lawnmower, hand mixer, drill, dishwasher, air conditioner, electric toothbrush, stereo, organ, etc.

Put the following on the chalk board:

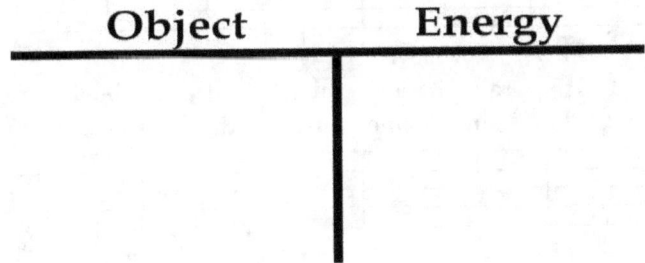

Have the children try and guess what the sounds come from and what type of energy does it take to make them operate.

Mary K. Payne

ACTIVITY THREE: Rain, a Natural Resource

What type of energy does rain provide? Hydroelectric power plants. The water turns the turbines and this generates energy.

Step I

Begin this activity by explaining how rain is a natural source of energy. Put these statements on the board and discuss each.

    1. The rain falls and collects in rivers.
    2. The rivers run into the reservoirs.
    3. The water flows through the dam and turns the turbines and this makes electricity.

Step II

Teaching an energy-related song.

Music with Feelings

1. Write words to the song on the board.

2. Teach the first line of *It Rained A Mist* by singing it to them a couple of times. Then let them try to sing it, gradually continuing to the next three lines.

3. Divide the children into five groups so they may dramatize the rain, the sun, the grass, the flowers, and the chorus. If have found that it is hard for the children to act, play instruments, and sing at the same time. Each group can cut whatever he represents out of construction paper and pin it on the front of him. (The fifth graders even like to act out these songs.)

4. Give each group the following instruments:

>   Triangle - rain
>   cymbals - sun
>   rhythm sticks - grass
>   sand blocks - flowers

Step III - The Rain

This is another song that will get them in the mood for learning about energy. Children enjoy moving around during music. Since most of the activities will be taught from their desks, the last activity needs to be more active.

1. Sing the song two times to the students.

2. Write the words on the board. (It is better to sing short songs like this first, and then write it on the board.)

3. Have the children read the words.

4. Everyone sing together.

5. Have children clap to the rhythm.

6. Now have them run (R) to the eight notes, walk (W) to the half notes, and (H) hop to the quarter notes.

Step IV - Rain Dance

1. Divide children into two groups, chorus and dancers.

2. Help children compose a rain dance (circle form).

3. Have chorus sing or chant while other dance.

ACTIVITY FOUR - Energy Poems

A food chain begins with a green plant, then the animals eat the plants, and the people then eat the animals. The bacteria and worms are the last link that cleans up the world.

This lesson will be an example to show the children how to write a poem and put it to music. The poem should express just one idea pertaining to energy. Put the children in five groups and have them help each other. Have the children listen to this example and guess what tune you are using. Write the song on the board. Now have them sing it all together.

Example

Tune: *Twinkle, Twinkle, Little Star*

> The plants are dying all today.
> Tell me, is there another way?
> What will happen when they die?
> Will this finally make us cry?
> When the plants die, you will see
> Nothing living, including me.

Now put some key energy words on the blackboard to give the children something to get them started. Also suggest some tunes that they can use to put their poem to music such as *Mary Had a Little Lamb* and *Old McDonald Had A Farm*. Sing both tunes for them. Most children in fifth grade will know these tunes. Some key words to put on the board include:

- solar
- energy
- coal
- gas
- oil
- sun

Concluding the Lesson

Have each group sing their poem to the class. Discuss with the class, after each presentation, what their song taught us.

First, ask the children to answer these questions about the song that was the example.

1. Why do people die if there are no plants?

2. How would you feel if you knew you were going to die?

3. What will happen if we run out of energy?

4. How can we save energy?

5. How do you think a plant feels when it doesn't get enough sunlight?

Predicted Outcome

From having been exposed to these facts about energy, I hope to have made these children become more energy conscious. They may remember to turn off the lights more often when leaving a room.

Resources to Help with Lessons

Miscellaneous Ideas

1. Children like to dress up into costumes. A good way to make music more interesting is to use different hats, when acting out a song. Crepe paper strips and other paraphernalia such as scarves are also useful and inexpensive. Finger, paper, hand, and stick puppets are logs of fun, too.

2. A good way to review the lines and spaces on the treble clef is by using your hand. All the fingers are the lines and all the spaces in between the fingers and thumb are the spaces. Turn your hand side-ways and point to one of the lines or spaces. Then choose a child to tell you the answer.

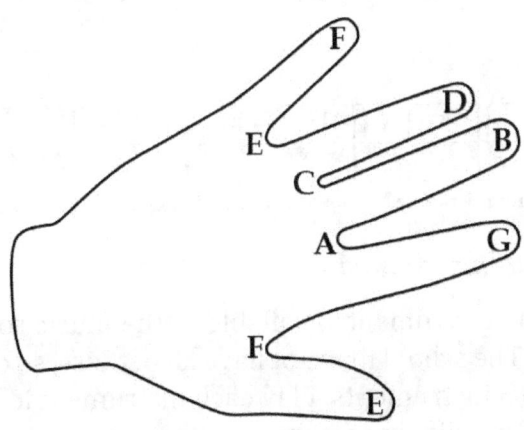

Mary K. Payne

Warm-ups

Warm-ups are activities used to get the children acquainted with each other. They can also be used as motivators. My favorite warm-up is sung on two notes. It is sung all on the same note, except for six notes and they go up one step. The song can be started on any pitch and sound like it should. The underlined words are the notes that go up. This activity can be used for second through sixth grades.

> Round in a circle,
> *Let's* play a game,
> All you do is *say* your name
> And *the beat* goes on.

Now point to any child and have him sing their name, for example, *Peg*-gy Kirk.

Another good warm-up is for listening skills. The teacher should clap her hands to different beats. Clap sometimes loud and sometimes soft. This activity can be used in any elementary grade.

Clap the number of beats shown above each note while counting 1-2-3-4 time.

Rhythm Band Instruments

There may be instruments available in the music room or kept in the office. The school may not have all of these, so choose your favorite 10-15 instruments. Play each instrument in order to let them hear the different sounds. Showing and playing the instruments will motivate the students when writing reports about their favorite instrument.

Also, some of the instruments may be used in some of the activities in the book. Here is a list of instruments: Flute,

Flutophone, Ukelele, Chromatic Melody Bells, Guitar, Oriental Gone, Hand Bell, Maracas, Recorder, Diatonic Step Bells, Copper Cowbells, Wood Blocks, Rhythm Sticks, Triangle, Sand Blocks, Tone Blocks, Cymbals and Finger Cymbals, Rhythm Claves, Castanets, Tambourines.

About the Author

Mary K. Payne graduated from San Jacinto College with an Elementary Music Degree in 1971. She then graduated from the University of Houston with a Bachelor's Degree in Elementary Education in 1974 followed by a Master's degree in 1978. She also earned a Special Education Certificate in 1985 from University of Houston Clear Lake. She has taught regular, special, and bilingual education classes in every grade from 1st to 12th for 39 years. After retiring, she still finds time to tutor students and consult parents.

A talented singer, she has sung *The Star-Spangled Banner* for the past 27 years as part of the opening ceremonies for Houston Astros Baseball games. She is the mother of two grown children and has two grandchildren. Her love for children and music inspired her to write this helpful book.

www.ingramcontent.com/pod-product-compliance
Lightning Source LLC
Chambersburg PA
CBHW050447010526
44118CB00013B/1725